KIM MORRISSEY

Kim Morrissey is a Canadian playwright and poet. She has
published two books of poetry: *Batoche* (Coteau Books, 1989,
reprinted 1990, 1992) and *Poems for Men Who Dream of
Lolita* (Coteau Books, 1992). *Batoche* is a suggested text for
Canadian secondary schools, and both books are taught in
universities in Canada, England, Germany and Denmark. She is
currently working on *Clever as Paint*, a play about the Pre-
Raphaelite painter/poets Elizabeth Siddal, Dante Gabriel
Rossetti and William Morris, for Simon Hewitt's Anabasis
Theatre.

A Selection of Other Volumes in this Series

*Published by Theatre Communications Group, distributed by Nick Hern Books

KIM MORRISSEY

DORA

A Case of Hysteria

NICK HERN BOOKS
London

A Nick Hern Book

Dora first published in Great Britain in 1994
as a paperback original by Nick Hern Books Limited,
14 Larden Road, London W3 7ST

Front cover illustration: detail of a print showing Charcot
lecturing on hysteria at La Salpêtrière.

Typeset by Country Setting, Woodchurch, Kent TN26 3TB

Printed by Cox and Wyman Ltd, Reading, Berks

A CIP catalogue record for this book is available from
the British Library

ISBN 1 85459 295 5

Hysteria [histeer Ri-a], n. of or from the womb; (psych) a nervous disorder arising from repression, characterized by disassociation and producing physiological symptoms;
(coll.) a violent outburst of emotion.

For Roy

Introduction

Arising from all the popular and critical debate about Freud –
his views on sexuality, his unstated views on women, the
feminist retake on his work – Freud himself has gained in
stature, been inflated to dirigible proportions, if only at times as
a target. Kim Morrissey shoots him down, or at least deflates
him, brings him back to size – if not to earth – with her play,
Dora: a Case of Hysteria. With and through the play, she draws
on both Freud's writings and the more recent writing about
them to show what is not said in his case histories: his own
viewpoint and sexual fantasies inscribed in his interpretations
of dreams, and his 'readings' of character through sexuality.

In her play, *Dora: a Case of Hysteria*, Kim Morrissey brings
one of Freud's most notorious patients to life: she offers a
portrait of Dora as a likeable, sympathetic figure, and depicts
Freud himself as the figure with an over-active imagination.
The play thus becomes a case study of one of his case studies:
a joke about the unconscious desires and impulses inscribed in
Freud's own fantasy of Dora.

Would the real Dora please stand up? But of course, she can't.
Dora was the pseudonym Freud chose for a young middle-class
woman who was his 'patient' in 1900. Dora, with the nervous
cough and migraines, diagnosed by Freud as an 'hysteric'.
Dora, who told Freud of her confused familial arrangement – of
a father having an affair with another woman, that woman's
husband having made a play for Dora herself – but whose
'nervous disorder' was diagnosed as being related to Dora's
own confused sexuality, and what Freud viewed as her 'weakness' in her attraction to her father's mistress. The Pelican
series on Sigmund Freud (paperback edition of Volume 8,
Case Histories I: 'Dora' and 'Little Hans', reprinted in 1977),
is remarkably unselfconscious in its representation of Dora as
Freud himself saw her:

'Dora', an unhappy eighteen-year-old hysteric, was treated
by Freud in 1900. The case illustrated the value of dream
interpretation in treatment. Analysis of 'Dora's' dreams
revealed a complicated web of emotions – love, hatred and
jealousy – which had been so deeply repressed that she was
unaware of them. As Freud says, 'We are obliged to pay as
much attention in our case histories to the purely human and
social circumstances of our patients as to the somatic data and
the symptoms of the disorder. Above all our interest will be
directed towards the family circumstances . . .

The book jacket description describes Dora in the first sentence
as an 'hysteric', taking Freud's view of Dora as read: he was
the Doctor, she was the patient. But feminist critics have not
been patient with Freud's version of Dora's story. In fact, Dora
has only recently come to life as a character in her own right
since feminist critics and writers began to analyse Freud's
methods of analysis, to question his mode of questioning, to
study his language and the assumptions ingrained in his way
of seeing women: a white middle-class Jewish man's view of
women, situated in nineteenth century Vienna.

When feminist critics asked the question, 'what would Dora
have to say for herself if she had a voice?', they effectively
gave her a voice, or many voices: a myriad of possible perspectives which reveal, not necessarily a divided self in Dora, but
rather a complicated web of readers and writers, storytellers
and listeners, doctors and patients, desires and interpretations.

The Pelican book jacket accepts Freud's Dora as a matter of
fact. But Kim Morrissey frames Dora as a fictional character,
and looks consciously and critically at the unselfconscious
view of women captured in both Freud's perspective and
the book jacket which would enshrine it as 'truth'. Morrissey
reframes Dora, comparing her with other such female figures
previously seen through the eyes of men but now – with
the insights of feminist theory – well positioned for re-
representation. What recent feminist writing about Freud and
other of the 'great dead men' has revealed is the tendency to
stereotype women in terms of sexual categories, playing with

the Biblical Virgin/Whore dichotomy in ever-more subtle but no more liberating ways. Yet Dora, the woman who went to Freud for treatment, was a person, though we will never know precisely who, for we have only Freud's account. Freud's Dora – the Frankenstein monster he both created and (mis)represented – is now a major figure: an archetype of the hysterical woman if his view is to be believed, or if it is not, then an ambiguous female whose story is yet to be told, and retold, by and for each new generation looking for reflections of self images of women in history and myth.

In her attempt to tell Dora's story from Dora's point of view, Morrissey has cleverly targeted another nineteenth century man-who-created-women: Henrik Ibsen. Ibsen, a contemporary of Freud's, busily creating Nora – the woman who would slam the door on *A Doll's House* on a stage not far away – while Freud created his version of Dora. The similarity in the names is convenient and also the stuff of comedy in Morrissey's version. Morrissey was fascinated, in the research that led to the play, to find that Freud was not impressed, to say the least, with Ibsen and with socialists in general – this discovery helped to focus the play for her, by allowing her to do away with the assumption that the 'fathers of modern thought' could all be lumped together. Acknowledging a distance between Ibsen and Freud gave Morrissey fuel for comic commentary; Morrissey's Freud calls Dora 'Nora', in repeated 'Freudian slips' – only one of many instances in the play when Freud's theories are shown to reveal a great deal about himself – as if he is subconsciously associating the real woman who was his patient with the fictional characters created before her, and after her, by other men with other agendas. Dora was no more 'real' for Freud than was Ibsen's Nora, Morrissey implies. The women in these fictions (and Morrissey sees both Ibsen's play and Freud's case study as in essence, fictional) are symbols, and Morrissey is keen to show both how much, and how little, they have in common with each other, and with women alive and breathing and acting today.

Here, of course, Morrissey draws heavily, though indirectly, on feminist theory as it has been applied to Freud's life and work.

The feminist approach to Freud has been influential, in academic scholarship and in the effects it has had on popular culture and everyday life. But while feminist writing about psychoanalysis has contributed a great deal to contemporary debates about sexuality and representation, many students have been mystified by the language in which the theory is expressed. In the theatre, rather than the lecture hall or classroom, some of these ideas have taken their most accessible form. In the theatre, Ibsen's Nora does slam the door on the doll's house; and in the theatre, different Doras also come to life and shake up expectations of what women are or 'should be', slamming doors of other kinds and causing all manner of reverberations, real and symbolic.

In *Dora: a Case of Hysteria*, we are offered one portrait of Dora. The first, and best-known feminist portrait was that created by Hélène Cixous in her play *Portrait de Dora*, directed by Simone Benmussa (first produced at the Petit Orsay Theatre, Paris, February 1976). Both Cixous's and Morrissey's plays open with reference to 'the scene by the lake', wherein Mr. K. – a friend of the family and the husband of Dora's father's mistress, Frau K – makes a sexual advance on Dora. Or at least, so Dora says; so she believes. Both Cixous and Morrissey believe her, though Freud did not. The sessions with Freud focus on unravelling this mystery, or what actually happened, what Dora thinks of sex, what she wanted to happen, who stands for whom in the dreams and memories which Dora recounts. Here begins the story of Dora, from a contemporary feminist perspective. But of course there is not one feminist perspective, and Cixous herself has questioned the term 'feminist' in relation to her life and work, pointing out that the term has a specific meaning in France, not readily applicable to British and American definitions of feminism(s). Yet despite the labels approved by either author, both plays can be played for feminist impact.

The two plays differ in one very important respect. Cixous's *Portrait de Dora* represents Dora's attachment to Frau K as a lesbian attraction, a powerful and largely one-sided pull towards the beautiful, independent, sexual, older woman. In his analysis of Dora's attraction to Frau K, Freud was dismissive: this was a moment of weakness on her part. But for Cixous, it is the spark of strength – the true sign of her character and her awakening sexuality. Morrissey emphasizes something else: the comedy of Freud's interpretation. Whether or not Dora was, or would be, lesbian is not so interesting, in Morrissey's view, as the way in which Freud gives himself away by interpreting the lesbian attraction as a weakness. In revealing this view of weakness, Freud reveals the limits of his own thought (as feminist critics have shown in more 'serious' contexts). So Morrissey's play enacts feminist theory on Freud, as does Cixous's, taking the same moment but showing it up from different angles, with different agendas.

Both Cixous and Morrissey focus on key moments in the case study: Freud's dismissal of Dora's mother as insignificant – without even meeting her – is indicative, again, of his view of women: what he sees as women's marginality and weakness (to be taken for granted, at the word of men). The absent mother is translated into a shadowy presence in performance: she never appears, but seems to be lingering offstage, always about to enter, or to speak through Dora's voice. Similarly, both plays seize on the linguistic imperative of sex – the importance which Freud places on talking about sexuality. In Morrissey's version, this emphasis on 'naming sex' is played for comic effect, in a series of moments in which the joke is on Freud's own obsessions with 'talking dirty', whether or not he is actually, as he claims to be, doing so for Dora's sake. Freud probes Dora for information about the scene by the lake, suspecting that Dora experienced and was frightened into silence by what he assumes to be Mr. K's substantial erection. But Morrissey's Freud gets excited by his own thoughts and words as he talks sexy to Dora; Freud 'gets off', to put it crudely, on this analysis session. Freud becomes the focus of the scene and Dora – what happened to her, what she saw, thought, felt and might need to talk about – is shunted to the periphery, along with the influence of Dora's invisible mother. But the scene is comic, not only due to the dialogue but mainly because Dora is not portrayed as a victim, but rather as a wise and ironic listener to Freud; the roles are reversed.

Morrissey's Dora does not deflate Cixous's Dora. Each gains something from reflection in and on the other. Both might have been. We'll never know, but it is exciting and intriguing to play the two Doras off one another, and it is rewarding to see two female figures in drama, created by women and directed by women. Of course, both Cixous and Morrissey invest in Dora words and views shaped by their own positions, views, perspectives on psychoanalysis, drama and sexuality. The authors, and directors, and critical/theoretical backgrounds are very much 'alive' in both plays. Reading the two together, the reader is left, not with a question as to which one 'Dora really was', but with the reassuring possibility that she was both, or neither; that she would, if she could, represent herself quite differently. To the extent that Freud's theories do hold true in a general sense, even Dora's portrait of Dora might not give us the 'whole picture'.

The strength of Cixous' play is its dark, complex, poetic language, its imagery and insight, its elegant and eloquent silences and omissions in the stream of consciousness dialogues which overlap and flow from one character to another. The strength of Morrissey's play is its use of contemporary, everyday language, its use of Freud as an unreliable narrator, and its deliberate silences, timed, as if in stand-up comedy to pack the most punch. Morrissey's play is a black comedy, and this approach reveals another side to Dora, and offers a different key to the reticule we've all heard so much about (and if you haven't already, you will in these pages). Sexuality *is* the key, as Freud insisted, and as Cixous and other thinkers and writers have since questioned, considered and restated. Now Morrissey offers another perspective, another view of the 'key' to understanding Dora, understanding sexuality, understanding the representation of women. Morrissey works through humour. In light-hearted style, Morrissey leads us once again into what is now familiar territory, but takes us around the halls of the funhouse in a different direction, and teaches us to laugh as we go.

This is a play for actors and students and those interested in experimenting with what the text does and does not say, on the stage and on the page. It enriches the study of Freud, and adds to the study of Cixous' *Portrait de Dora*. It encourages laughter on the tangled and complicated subject of sexuality – no mean feat in these plague-ridden times. It offers one way into the story of Dora, while allowing for any number of others to be created, played, replayed, performed and published.

Lizbeth Goodman
Cambridge, October 1993

Suggestions for Further Reading

Hélène Cixous, 'Portrait of Dora', published in Playscripts 91: *Benmussa Directs*: 'Portrait of Dora' by Helen Cixous, and 'The Singular Life of Albert Nobbs' by Simone Benmussa. London: John Calder; Dallas: Riverrun Press, 1979, translated by Anita Burrows.

Hélène Cixous, 'Portrait of Dora', published in *Diacritics, Special Issue on Dora*, Spring 1983, translated by Sarah Burd.

Mary Jacobus, ed., *Reading Woman: Essays in Feminist Criticism*. New York: Columbia University Press, 1986.

Juliet Mitchell, *The Longest Revolution: on Feminism, Literature and Psychoanalysis*. New York: Pantheon Books, 1983; London: Virago, 1984.

Angela Richards, ed., *The Pelican Freud Library, Volume 3: Sigmund Freud and Joseph Breuer: Studies on Hysteria*. Harmondsworth: Penguin, 1974.

Angela Richards, ed., *The Pelican Freud Library, Volume 4: The Interpretation of Dreams*. Harmondsworth: Penguin, 1975.

Angela Richards, ed., *The Pelican Freud Library, Volume 6: Jokes and Their Relation to the Unconscious*. Harmondsworth: Penguin, 1976.

Angela Richards, ed., *The Pelican Freud Library, Volume 8: Case Histories I: 'Dora' and 'Little Hans'*. Harmondsworth: Penguin, 1977.

Jean Strouse, ed., *Women and Analysis: Dialogues on Psychoanalytic Views of Femininity*. Boston: G.K. Hall and Co., 1985.

Chronology: Freud

1856	May 6, born in Moravia.
1873	Enters Vienna University as a medical student.
1881	Graduates as Doctor of Medicine.
1884-7	Researches the clinical uses of cocaine.
1886	Marriage to Martha Bernays.
1887	Birth of Mathilde.
1887	Friendship and correspondence with Wilhelm Fliess, until 1902.
1889	Birth of Martin.
1891	Birth of Oliver.
1892	Birth of Ernst.
1893	Birth of Sophie.
1895	Birth of Anna.
1895	*Studies on Hysteria* published, with Breuer.
1897	Abandons theory of infantile seduction.
1900	*Interpretation of Dreams* published.
1901	Jan. 24, case study of 'Dora' offered for publication.
1901	*The Psychopathology of Everyday Life* published.
1902	Appointed Professor Extraordinarius.
1905	'Dora' case study published.
1920	Death of Sophie.
1923	Diagnosed as having cancer of the jaw.
1924	'Dora' case study revised and reissued.
1938	Hitler's invasion of Austria.
1939	Sept. 23, dies in London.

Chronology: Dora

1882   Nov. 1, 'Dora' (Ida Bauer) born in Vienna. (Charles Bernheimer and Claire Kahane, eds., *In Dora's Case* (New York: Columbia University Press, 1990).

1894   Following the advice of his friend 'Herr K', Dora's father Philip is treated by Freud for syphilis, and 'cured'.

1898   Summer, 'Dora' is brought, reluctantly, to Freud to be cured of her cough. Freud proposes psychological treatment, the proposal is not accepted.

1900   Oct., begins treatment with Freud, which lasts less than twelve weeks.

1900   Dec. 31, New Year's Eve, breaks off treatment.

1901   Jan. 1, the twentieth century begins.

1901   Jan. 25, Freud writes to Fliess, telling him he has finished writing the case study. The case study has been written from memory, at the end of the treatment. Freud sends it off for publication immediately. The case study, though it does not name anyone, mentions the age of Dora, and her only sibling, and gives intimate details about her family circle: her mother is a compulsive house-cleaner; her father is a small manufacturer; he suffered from detached retina in 1882; he came to Freud in 1894 to be cured of syphilis; Freud also knew Dora's father's sister (who was a little older than her brother) who had had an unhappy marriage and had died of a marasmus; Dora's father's older brother was a hypochondrial bachelor; in 1895 Dora stayed in Vienna with her aunt's family after the death of her aunt, and fell ill with appendicitis.

1902   Visits Freud, asking to resume treatment. Freud declines.

1903   Marries a composer.

1905	Freud publishes the case-study in *Monatsschrift fur Psychiatrie und Neurologie*, Bd. xxviii, Heft 4, 1905. Reprinted in Freud, *Sammlung kleiner, Schriften ii*, 1909.
19??	Birth of her son (and only child).
1912	Her mother Kathe dies of tuberculosis.
1913	Her father dies of tuberculosis.
1914	Her brother Otto marries.
1914-34	Otto becomes one of the principal leaders of the Austrian Socialist Party.
1922	According to Felix Deutsch, M.D. (husband of the more famous Karen) she visits him twice for treatment.
1923	Freud adds to his text's 'Clinical Picture', noting that a colleague (Deutsch) had easily recognised the patient as the Dora of '1899'.
1930s	Leaves Vienna, moves to France, and eventually to the United States (Deutsch).
1932	Her husband dies of coronary disease (Deutsch).
1938	Hitler's invasion of Austria.
1938	Her brother Otto dies of coronary disease (Deutsch).
1945	Dies of colonic cancer in New York City, survived by her son.
1957	Deutsch writes 'A Footnote to Freud's "Fragment of an Analysis of a Case of Hysteria",' first published in *Psychoanalytic Quarterly*, 26 (1957), 159-167, claiming to have examined 'Dora' in 'the late fall of 1922'. He gets her age wrong, and the essay contains further biographical details which are at odds with the biographical details given by the editors of *In Dora's Case*. Deutsch describes her as chatting with him 'in a flirtatious manner' in 1922, and offers other details of her life, death and personality. His New York informant said she had 'slighted and tortured' her husband who 'had preferred to die . . . rather than divorce her'; that she had been 'one of the most repulsive hysterics' Deutsch's informant had ever met. Dora's impressions of Freud, Deutsch, and Deutsch's informant are not recorded.

Author's Note

I have profited variously and gratefully by the reading of
Freud's *Fragment of a Case of Hysteria* (1905), Freud's letters,
particularly his correspondence with Wilhelm Fliess, the
biography of Freud by Ernest Jones, Lucy Freedman's *Freud
and Women*, Jane Gallup's *Feminism and Freud*, Harris and
Harris's *The One-Eyed Doctor: Sigmund Freud* and Joseph
Wortis's *Fragment of an Analysis with Freud*.

Acknowledgements

The playwright would like to thank the Canada Council
and the Saskatchewan Arts Board for their continued support
and assistance on this and other projects. A scene from *Dora*
appeared in *Grain* and *Gairfish*, and an earlier version in
Canadian Theatre Review.

First workshopped by Saskatchewan Playwrights Centre
Saskatoon, Saskatchewan, October 1985.

First produced by Wheatland Theatre, Regina, Saskatchewan,
February 27-March 15, 1987, directed by Steve Gregg.
Set design: Kate Gregg.

DORA   Kim Nedoborski
FREUD   Jim Timmins
PAPA   Greg Morley

Produced by BBC Radio Three, and broadcast November 19,
1991, directed by Cherry Cookson.

DORA   Lesley Sharp
FREUD   Clive Merrison
PAPA   Edward De Souza

Produced by OTC at Hen and Chickens Theatre,
London, England, March 17-April 10, 1993, directed
by Christine Hoodith. Set design: Maddy Morris.
Stage manager: Greta Dowling.

DORA   Joanne McInnes
FREUD   Barry Shannon
PAPA   Simon Hewitt

Characters

DORA (between ages of 16 and 20)
FREUD (mid-forties)
PAPA (mid-forties)

Setting: Vienna, 1900

ACT ONE

FREUD *enters.*

FREUD. Good evening, Gentlemen. (*Bows, clicks heels.*)

There are certain so-called critics of psychotherapy – thankfully not among us – who regard a case study as a frivolous excuse for salacious or pornographic gossip . . . a roman à clef – a romance – told entirely for their own entertainment. These critics will be disappointed tonight, I assure you. No clues remain as to this young girl's identity – even her name has been changed.

Our subject tonight we shall call . . . Dora . . . A young girl in the first flush of youth. Her family has just recently moved to Vienna. Her father is a small manufacturer, her mother, a compulsive house-cleaner, and she has one brother, one-and-a-half years her senior, now a well-known (*With distaste.*) socialist leader.

I first saw Nora as a child of –

– I beg your pardon – 'Dora' – I'm afraid Herr Ibsen has ruined poor 'Nora' for us forever – . . .

Yes, Dora . . . a young girl blossoming with intelligence, and charming good looks . . .

Lights up on DORA *waltzing with child's music box playing a Viennese waltz,* PAPA *joins her for dance.*

FREUD. A young girl, critics say . . . and you are discussing bodily functions and sexual organs? Gentlemen. As you know, although I give bodily organs and processes their technical names, I introduce no information of which the patient is not already aware. This is not pornographic, but necessary, even when young girls are involved.

DORA. Don't be silly . . . I am only a child.

DORA and PAPA *exit, music box still playing.*

FREUD (*watches* DORA *exit*). And Gentlemen, I assure you, j'appelle un chatte une chatte.

So. Dora. The Clinical Picture.

I first saw Dora as a child, four years after I cured her father of a – specific – infection. Since I have found the off-spring of luetics are susceptible to neuropsychoses, I was not in the least surprised to hear his daughter had developed neurotic symptoms –

PAPA *knocks and enters, with* DORA, *aged 14.*

FREUD (*to* PAPA). Ah, good day! (*To* AUDIENCE.) Dora was fourteen at the time, and unmistakably neurotic.

PAPA. Good day, Sigmund.

FREUD. And (*Not sure of the name.*) – Dora, is it? . . .

DORA *nods shyly.*

Yes, Dora.

DORA (*politely*). Good morning, Herr Doctor.

FREUD. Herr *Professor.*

DORA (*coughs nervously*). Herr Professor.

FREUD. And how are you today?

DORA. Fine, Herr Professor.

FREUD. And how is the cough?

PAPA. Worse, much worse.

FREUD (*to* PAPA). Come, come. You know I conclude nothing from the accounts of relatives.

Abruptly waves PAPA *away.*

You may go.

PAPA *clicks heels together politely, bows, exits.*

FREUD (*treats* DORA *like a specimen*). According to her father, the patient had developed neurotic symptoms by the age of eight: bedwetting, thumb-sucking, chronic dyspnoea. By the age of twelve, in 1894, the same year her father came to me for treatment, she began to suffer one-sided – or more precisely, half-sided – which is to say – unilateral head-aches – (*Note: Dora pronounces 'mama' and 'papa' with the accent on the last syllable.*)

DORA. Like my Papa.

FREUD. No. Not like your Papa. (*To* AUDIENCE.) Unilateral headaches –

DORA. *Exactly* like Papa . . .

FREUD. – in the nature of a migraine . . .

DORA. . . . *And* nervous coughing.

FREUD (*corrects her*). Tussis nervosa.

DORA. *And* I lose my voice. And dear Papa said –

FREUD. Sit down please.

DORA. But Papa . . .

FREUD. Sit down. Sit down. This is my lecture, young lady. Not yours . . .

DORA *sits.*

FREUD. Gentlemen: The best way of talking about sexual matters with young girls is to be dry and direct. In this way, it is possible for a man to speak to both girls and women about sexual subjects of all kinds without harming them . . . and without laying himself open to suspicion. The key is to convince them it is unavoidable.

(*To* DORA.) Dora, everything said here – to me – and me to you – must be strictly confidential. Do you understand?

DORA *nods.*

FREUD. Excellent. Excellent. The key to your hysteria and your recovery lies locked within your own memories, guilty dreams, and hidden activities. Before we are through you will see that your headaches, your coughing, your vaginal discharges, indeed all your supposed illnesses, are nothing more than an acting out – a wedding, as it were, of your secret phantasies, dreams, and sexual desires. There's no need to feel guilty or feel shame. You must admit all, for there is no such thing as an unconscious 'No.' The more you deny, the more I know it is true –

DORA (*frightened*). Papa! Papa!

DORA *runs out.*

FREUD (*shakes head*). As you see – unmistakably neurotic.

Although I proposed treatment at that time, my proposal was not accepted – excuse me . . . adopted – since her symptoms passed off.

Nonetheless, she continued to cause her parents a great deal of grief. By the age of sixteen, she was unmistakably neurotic: she suffered from depression, irritability and irreverence. She was on bad terms with her mother, refused to do her share of the house work, avoided proper social intercourse, and insisted on attending lectures for women!

One day her poor parents were heart-broken to find on her writing desk, or inside it, a letter taking leave of life.

FREUD *takes letter from desk.* DORA *enters, aged 16.*

DORA. How on earth did you get that? It was locked up in my desk!

FREUD. Never mind how I got it.

Holds letter and cigar in air away from DORA.

DORA. Isn't anything private? Don't I have anything of my own?

FREUD. You know very well you left this letter there on purpose, to punish your parents.

DORA. But it was in *my* writing desk. And my writing desk was *locked.*

FREUD. Of course. You locked it deliberately, to pique their curiosity.

DORA. Don't you understand? It's *my* letter. It was in *my* writing-desk. It was locked with *my* key. You had no right. You have no right at all.

FREUD. Don't shout, young lady. It is your father's writing-desk, not yours. He bought it.

DORA. Papa! Papa! Papa come here! Papa how could you!

PAPA (*off-stage*). But my little treasure, my dear, we were so worried, we thought it was best . . .

DORA (*partly off-stage*). It was none of your business . . . I don't care . . . I hate you! I hate you I hate you I hate you! And I'll never forgive you for this . . . Never!

DORA *exits completely, slamming door.*

FREUD. One day, after a slight passage of words with her father, Nora had her first fit of delirious convulsions. In spite of her objections –

DORA (*aged 18, pulled onto stage by* PAPA). Will you let go!

PAPA. Dora! . . . Don't be rude . . . Come along . . . Be quiet! . . .

DORA. I won't! I won't! You'll have to kill me first.

PAPA (*grimly*). Don't tempt me.

DORA. Oh Papa! How can you say such a thing . . . Don't you love me any more?

PAPA. There, there . . . there, there . . . of course I do.

DORA. As much as you love Mama?

PAPA. Of course, more, much more, My Little Princess.

FREUD. The Oedipal Complex yet again.

DORA. As much as Frau K?

PAPA. Dora!

FREUD. What's this? Frau K? Herr K's wife? (PAPA *nods reluctantly.*) What about Frau K?

DORA. Papa adores her.

PAPA. Dora, don't be silly. (*To* FREUD.) Frau K is simply a friend . . . a good friend . . . a very good friend . . . As you know, we made the K's acquaintance at the Hotel at The Lake.

DORA. When I was ten, and Papa's eyes were bad.

FREUD. Yes. (*To* AUDIENCE, *a footnote.*) Detached retina. 1892. Go on.

PAPA. What more can I say? Frau K nursed me through my long illness.

DORA. She used to sit with him all day long in a dark bedroom, and they blocked up the key-hole!

PAPA. – To screen the light from the door. Very bad for the eyes.

DORA. And sometimes she forbade my Mama to come in!

PAPA. Again, for the eyes.

DORA. And once, when Mama wanted to change the sheets, she found the door locked!

PAPA. My wife is very insistent.

FREUD. Of course, of course . . . (*To* AUDIENCE, *a footnote.*) Though I have never met Dora's mother, the girl and her father led me to think of her as an ignorant and exceedingly silly woman –

DORA. Stupid old cow.

FREUD (*continuing the footnote*) – A typical example of 'housewife's psychosis'.

PAPA. Exactly. She kept wanting to change the sheets, Lord knows why.

FREUD. Such obsessional washing is common amongst housewives.

DORA. But Frau K said –

FREUD. Ah! Frau K. Go on.

PAPA. There's really nothing to tell. She is a great friend of the family; in fact, so friendly that Dora insists on spending all her holidays with the K's at The Lake.

DORA. Not any more.

PAPA (*grimly*). Yes you will.

DORA. No I won't.

PAPA. Yes she *will* . . . Dora positively worships Frau K, and as for Herr K – well . . .

DORA. He's a dirty old man.

FREUD (*to* DORA). Not so old, surely. I know Herr K.

DORA. Old as Papa! Old as You!

FREUD (*to* DORA). In the prime of life!

DORA. *And* he made me an immoral proposal by The Lake.

PAPA. He didn't.

DORA. He did . . . He did!

PAPA (*to* FREUD). Sheer phantasy . . . Herr K assures me
nothing –

DORA (*to* PAPA). Are you calling me a liar? (*To* FREUD.)
Two years ago at The Lake he told me he wanted to –

FREUD (*to* DORA). That's enough, young lady.

PAPA (*whisper, to* FREUD). Please. I beg you. Try to cure her
of this hysterical phantasy. Poor Frau K is already most
unhappy with her husband, and you know I get nothing out
of my own wife . . .

FREUD (*whisper, to* PAPA). Let me see what I can do.

PAPA. Thank you . . . thank you.

PAPA *exits*.

FREUD. So, Dora, your father tells me you are accustomed to
laugh at your doctors . . . Hmmm, sit down.

DORA. No thank you, Herr Professor. I prefer to stand.

FREUD. Sit down . . . Young Lady, I know you have been
accustomed to laugh at your doctors, but you will not laugh
at me. . . . You have had hydrotherapy and electrical shock,
you have been put to bed for six months, you have been
forced to eat things you dislike, and perhaps you have even
been bled . . . And none of this has done any good, has it?

I am a new sort of doctor. I will not poke you, or probe you,
or administer electrical shocks. We will only talk, and after
awhile, you may begin to get well, and then possibly, if you
make progress, it might be possible for me to persuade your
father to give up your other doctors. Do you understand?

DORA. Just talk?

FREUD. Just talk. But you must tell me everything. Even if it is embarrassing or rude. Do you understand? Good. Now, when did you first notice this . . . dislike . . . of Herr K?

DORA. Oh, I don't know.

FREUD (*to* AUDIENCE). Note the phrase 'I don't know'. It is the phrase she will use every time she's about to confess to anything that has been repressed.

DORA. Well, he's been spying on me for years, but really, it was the proposal at The Lake two years ago that . . . No! wait! About four years ago, I didn't tell anyone, but –

FREUD. 1896. So you were fourteen.

DORA. Well, yes . . . I think so . . . thirteen or fourteen . . . Herr K and his wife and myself agreed to meet at his office to watch the church festival from his window. But when I arrived, Frau K was not there, and when I came in, he sent the clerks all away . . . (*Pause.*) Well? What do you think?

FREUD. Possibly it was lunchtime.

DORA. Well, yes, but I came late.

FREUD. Maybe they were behind in their work, and had to work into their lunch hour to make up.

DORA. But they didn't come back.

FREUD. How do you know? Did you stay all afternoon?

DORA. No, because of what happened after. And then he had the audacity two years later at The Lake to –

FREUD. Begin at the beginning. You are in his office. Correct. To watch a procession for a church festival. Right? Proceed.

DORA. Well, I waited and waited for Frau K to come, and he smoked, and just watched me . . . and then, when we couldn't wait any longer, because the procession was about to begin, he told me to wait for him by the door to the staircase, while he went up to pull down the shutters.

FREUD. To wait where?

DORA. At the door from the office to the staircase, leading up to the upper storey.

FREUD. And where is that?

DORA (*stands up*). Here is the office. Down there . . .
(*Gestures to* AUDIENCE.) . . . is the church square. Yes? . . .
Here is the Hallway, through the door to the office . . . Here
is the door to the stairway. Up there is the upper storey. He
goes to pull down the shutters to watch the procession. And
I am here. At the open door. And when he pulled down the
shutters to open them . . .

FREUD. I don't understand. Why does he have to pull *down*
the shutters? And where is *he*?

DORA. Why up, of course. Can't you see? Here. You be Herr
K. So you are here.

Pulls FREUD *into position.*

FREUD (*to* AUDIENCE, *a footnote*). Transference! 'I am Herr
K. Herr K is here!' Most patients take months to make such
a leap! Wonderful! (*To* DORA.) So I am upstairs.

DORA. Pulling down the shutters.

FREUD. And you are downstairs?

DORA. Waiting for you.

FREUD. And then?

DORA. And then you come down the stairs . . .

FREUD. I come down like this?

DORA. Slower . . . very slowly, and you are smoking.

FREUD. Like this?

DORA. Yes, but come down more slowly, because the light is
very dim, with the shutters drawn.

FREUD. Like this?

DORA. Yes, exactly . . . you come down the stairs smoking . . .
and then, instead of moving past me . . . into the office . . .

FREUD. What do I do?

DORA. You clasp me to you and you kiss me.

FREUD. And it's the first time.

DORA. The first time what?

FREUD. The first time you'd been kissed.

DORA. I was only a child.

FREUD. And I kissed you . . . on the brow?

DORA. On the mouth. On the mouth.

FREUD. And you like it, don't you.

DORA. No. No. I hate it. I hate that kiss . . . wet and flabby like
an old toad's lip. I hate it. I *hate* you. I hate you Herr K!
You disgust me.

FREUD. But you stay. You stay for the procession, don't
you . . . Don't you, Dora . . . Look at me.

DORA. No! I ran from the office. I ran down the street to my
home and I washed . . . I scrubbed and scrubbed until my
lips were red.

FREUD. But such a little kiss . . .

DORA. It disgusted me. I could still feel his lips burning on
mine, days after. Sometimes even now.

FREUD. And yet you didn't tell anyone.

DORA. How could I? . . . They would be so disgusted, and
they would blame *me*. They would think I must have done
something. But I didn't, Herr Professor . . . I didn't . . . did I?

FREUD. But Herr K is quite handsome. A young girl should
feel excited to be kissed by such a man, would she not?

DORA. No. I hate him. I hate his grey beard, and the way
his breath stinks of cigars. I hate him . . . And even if I
didn't . . . I was only a child . . . How was I to know? . . .
And then at The Lake two years later –

Beat.

FREUD. What did he do?

DORA. It wasn't what he did, it was what he said . . . he said
since he got nothing from his own wife, since Papa, he
thought it was only fair that – he said he wanted to –
I wanted to die . . . I wanted to crawl away and die!

FREUD. There, there . . .

FREUD (*to* AUDIENCE). So you see: Petit Hysteria.

Whatever occurred, or, as Dora's father insists, did not occur at The Lake two years later, we can only conclude that the behaviour of Dora at fourteen was already totally and completely hysterical. She declared she could still feel the pressure of Herr K's lips upon hers. But instead of the genital sensations which would be felt by a healthy girl, Dora felt only disgust. This disgust could not simply be physical revulsion – Herr K is in the prime of life and – some say – (*Preens.* HERR K *looks like* FREUD.) – remarkably handsome.

No. I think Dora felt not only his kiss on her lips, but also, in his stormy embrace, his erect member against her body. This perception was revolting; so revolting it was suppressed and replaced by the harmless sensation of pressure on her thorax. Hence the nervous coughing.

Of course, this could only be true if it could also be proved that Dora knew what a man's . . . that is . . . had been aware of Herr K's . . . could be forced to admit –

(*Starts again.*) To test this addendum to my theory, I questioned Dora cautiously . . . trying to discover if she knew the signs of physical excitement in a man's body.

(*To* DORA.) Dora . . .

DORA. Yes?

FREUD. Dora, did you notice anything else?

DORA. When?

FREUD. When he kissed you . . . when he said things . . . did he seem . . . different?

DORA. He seemed very excited.

FREUD. Excited . . . You mean Physically Excited?

DORA. Well, yes.

FREUD. So you *do* know the signs of a man who is Physically Excited?

DORA. Of course . . . Doesn't everyone?

FREUD. Everyone?

DORA. Well, don't they?

FREUD. Tell me. What are these . . . signs . . . of excitement . . . How can you tell?

DORA. Well, for one thing: you can tell by his mouth.

FREUD (*covers mouth*). By the mouth – how?

DORA. Well, when Herr K gets excited, he starts to spit when he talks.

FREUD. And that is all? That's the only way you can tell that he's excited? I mean, Physically Excited.

DORA. Well, of course, there are other things, too.

FREUD (*crosses legs*). What other things?

DORA. Well, I'd rather not say . . . Mama said it was rude.

FREUD. Forget Mama. Nothing is rude in this office. You must tell me . . . it is very important. Tell me exactly how you can tell Herr K is excited.

DORA (*embarrassed*). Well, he farts.

FREUD (*to* AUDIENCE, *lecturing*). Flatulence. Not unknown. Commonly a sign of nervous weakness. Note the case of Herr Von F . . . Budapest, 1894. (*To* DORA) . . . Go on.

DORA. That's all there is.

FREUD. Look at me, Dora. You did not notice his Member?

DORA. His what?

FREUD. His Member . . . his John Thomas . . . his Man Below Stairs . (DORA *looks blank.*) his Flagpole, his Wiener, his Schlong . . . his Penis . . . (*Impatient.*) His Peter, his Prick, his Cock. You did not notice?

DORA. Well... no.

FREUD. No?

DORA. No.

FREUD. But you know now, don't you. You know what a man's Member is, don't you?

DORA. Yes.

FREUD. And you felt it, did you . . . when he pressed you . . . When he pressed you by the staircase . . . when he pressed you by The Lake?

DORA. No! I didn't! I swear I didn't!

FREUD. You didn't feel it when he pressed you . . . When he pressed you here . . . or here . . .

DORA (*breaking away*). No I didn't! I didn't! I couldn't! I –

(*Surprise, then embarrassment.*) Oh dear – Excuse me. May I use your (*Embarrassed.*) . . . your . . .

FREUD. You mean the . . . ? Ah. Of course, of course!

DORA *exits.*

FREUD. Notice that from the very beginning I used the greatest care not to introduce the patient to any new information in the area of sexual knowledge. I only gave a thing a name when her references to it became so clear that there seemed to be very little risk in translating it into direct speech.

Note also the Widerstand, which is to say, the resistance to admitting physical contact took place. Such vigorous denial is often a symptom of repressed knowledge.

DORA *enters.*

Ah, Dora, back from the . . . ? (*Coughs.*)

DORA. Yes, Herr Professor . . . Shall I lie down on the couch?

FREUD. Do what ever you wish . . . Now Dora, when Herr K pressed his –

DORA (*sits on* FREUD's *desk*). No . . . I'm done with Herr K. I can see what's going on, you know. I'm not stupid. It's perfectly clear Papa and Frau K are having an affair. Mama must be blind not to see.

FREUD. What makes you think that?

DORA. Well, first there was the locked door . . . and then, the next summer, Papa made us all go on holidays together, and Frau K complained that her child kept her awake, and so she moved to the end of the hall.

FREUD. But what does that matter?

DORA. She moved *all alone* to the end of the hall . . . and after two days, Papa complained of the stuffiness, and then *he* moved to the end of the hall.

FREUD. So?

DORA. So their rooms shared a passage!

FREUD. But that isn't enough to think your father and Frau K would be . . .

DORA. And one day, Papa and Frau K came back from the woods, out of breath, and covered with leaves, and Papa said we children had every reason to be grateful to Frau K, and when Mama asked why, he said he was about to shoot himself, but Frau K had knocked him off-balance and thrown herself on the gun!

FREUD (*to* AUDIENCE). So that was the connection with Dora's own attempt at suicide!

(*To* DORA.) Frau K had thrown herself on the gun . . . And did you believe him?

DORA. Would you? . . . And when Mama told Auntie, Auntie laughed and called Frau K 'Hetty Gabler'.

But that's not all! Every summer, Papa coughs, and coughs, and complains, and then goes away without us . . . and every time he goes, sure enough, Frau K goes away too. And even moving to town . . . we move here, and three weeks later, we hear the K's have moved too! And last month, when Papa said he felt worse, and went away to the Hotel at The Lake, I found out that he and Frau K – You see that's what I hate: Papa is telling lies, and no matter how much I tell him he's hurting Mama, he still does as he pleases. He's so insincere . . . so hypocritical . . . Poor Mama! . . . And that isn't the worst: the worst is seeing him always on the street with Frau K. And Herr K is always on the street too. And it's disgusting, whenever he sees me, he turns to look at me.

FREUD. Herr K? How do you know?

DORA. Because he's so clumsy. Every time he turns to look, he keeps banging into something.

FREUD. But this doesn't mean he's looking at you. How do you know? Maybe he is glancing at your father.

DORA. But everytime he sees me alone, he follows me, to see where I'm going.

FREUD. But how do you know he's following you?

DORA. I can always tell it's Herr K because he gets so excited.

FREUD. You mean Physically Excited?

DORA (*mimics* FREUD). Yes 'Physically Excited'.

FREUD. And how can you tell he is Physically Excited?

DORA. Can I sit in your chair? . . .

Pause.

FREUD. How can you tell he is physically excited?

DORA. Well, when I walk down the street, I know he is following, because . . .

FREUD. Because? . . . Because?

DORA. Because I can hear him fart . . .

Well, what do you think?

FREUD. What do *you* think?

DORA. I think Papa is handing me over to Herr K, so he can spend more time with Frau K.

FREUD (*to* AUDIENCE). When a patient presents such a sensible and flawless argument, there is bound to be a moment of embarrassment for the doctor, which the patient may take advantage of. I was careful not to let Dora know that she was probably right in thinking that her father hadn't looked too closely into Herr K's behaviour, perhaps because of his own. But remember: the patient is using such arguments, which analysis can't attack, as a smoke-screen for hiding others, which it can . . .

DORA. Well?

FREUD (*to* DORA). I think you, yourself, have done precisely the same thing. Lie down.

DORA. What do you mean?

FREUD. You are an accomplice in your father's affair, are you not?

DORA. No!

FREUD. Yes. Lie down. Your father tells me you would never visit Frau K if you thought he was there . . . And furthermore, you had your old governess turned away.

DORA. No!

FREUD. Yes. Yes, Dora. Turned away! And why? For revenge. Because she was in love with your father.

DORA. No! Mama caught her stealing the silver –

FREUD (*interrupting on the word 'her'*). Yes, because she was in love with your father, and when he was there, she would be charming and intelligent, but when he was away . . . ah! And that's exactly the way you behave with Herr K's children, isn't it? Because she was in love with your father the way you are in love with Herr K!

DORA. But I'm not in love with Herr K! I loathe and detest him! Herr K disgusts me!

FREUD. Come, come, there's no need to be shy. No one will know, Dora; you can say anything you like within these four walls. Admit it. Admit this pretence at ill-health is just a trick learned from Frau K. Pretty little Frau K, with her adorable little cough.

DORA. But Frau K spits blood. And besides, she is in bad health whenever Herr K is at home.

FREUD. Whereas you are in bad health whenever Herr K is away! Exactly. And how long are these 'attacks' of ill-health?

DORA. A month, sometimes a month-and-a-half.

FREUD. And how long is Herr K away on his trips?

DORA. I don't know. Four weeks, maybe five or six.

FREUD. You see! Your illness reveals your love for Herr K, just as his wife's illness betrays her *dislike*.

DORA. But sometimes I'm sick when he's there.

FREUD. No doubt to wipe away the connection. And what of this aphonia? This loss of voice . . .

DORA. Well, sometimes, when I'm very ill, and my cough is very bad, my throat gets very sore and –

FREUD. Exactly. When the person you love is away you give up speaking; speech has no value since you cannot speak to *him*.

DORA. But I don't! I don't speak to him! I haven't spoken to him since The Lake.

FREUD. Ah! This Lake. This fantastic 'immoral proposal', which both your father and Herr K deny. Very well, Dora. What exactly was this proposal? What did he say? The truth, now.

DORA. Well, nothing.

FREUD. Nonsense. Widerstand. Resistance. What did he say? . . . What did you think he said?

DORA. I don't know.

FREUD. You don't know?

DORA. No! . . . I didn't let him finish. I gave him a box on the ear and ran away . . .

I don't know why, but Herr K has changed. The old Herr K would have rather died than tell a Lie, because Life must be lived Truly, in spite of the Small, Cowardly, Stupid, Nasty, Vindictive, Ungenerous, Mean-minded of the world. Without Truth, there is nothing.

When FREUD *can't stand the speech any longer, he whispers 'Ibsen'.*

FREUD. But why are you telling me this?

DORA. I don't know . . . Perhaps you're right. Perhaps I did used to love Herr K; I used to think I loved him; but I don't love him now. Not after all he's done to me. Not after he lied to Papa about The Lake, and Papa believed him.

And I don't care what anyone says, Papa has brought me here to have you tell me I am crazy to think he is having an affair with Frau K. But he is. He is in love with Frau K, and she's just using him, because he is a man of means.

FREUD (to AUDIENCE). Ah! Gentlemen, note her phrase: 'Man of means'. Behind this, lies its opposite: that her father, as a man, was *without* means – sexually speaking.

FREUD (*to* DORA, *thunders*). Young Lady, are you accusing your father of having a love affair with Frau K? You know your father is impotent. So if he is having an affair, how can he when he is impotent? And if he is impotent, how can he be having an affair? How do you account for the contradiction?

DORA (*tries to brazen it out*). Well, Mama always says there's more than one way to skin a cat.

FREUD (*to* AUDIENCE). J'appelle une chat une chat! (*Sternly.*) Dora, are you referring to other organs apart from the genitalia for sexual activity?

DORA (*puzzled*). . . . oh yes . . .

FREUD. You know what this means, don't you. You are thinking of precisely those parts of your body which are constantly inflamed.

DORA. I am?

FREUD. Yes. You know how the throat and mouth – the oral cavity, as they say – may be used in sexual intercourse with a man, don't you. There's no need to deny it, the more you deny, the more you give yourself away. Every time you cough, the tickling in your little throat excites you, doesn't it? Because every time it tickles and you cough, you imagine that act of sexual satisfaction between the two people whose affair constantly occupies your mind.

DORA. I don't think so.

FREUD. Yes you do, Dora.

DORA. I do?

FREUD. Yes. You forget I have talked to your father. I know
you have sucked your thumb as a child. I know you have
wet your bed to the age of eight. I know everything – even
your most secret, hidden, shameful thoughts and actions –

PAPA *knocks*.

FREUD. But don't be afraid. What is said between these four
walls is just between you and me. The relationship between
patient and doctor is strictly confidential. Say what you like,
no one will know. Not even your family. Do you
understand? Good.

PAPA *knocks again, and then enters.*

FREUD (*to* PAPA). Come in, come in. (*To* DORA.) Ah, Dora,
your father is here!

(*To* PAPA.) I think it would be best for her to come to me
five days a week.

PAPA. Excellent! Excellent!

FREUD. Very well, then. (*Checks appointments book.*)
Tomorrow. Ten o'clock, Dora?

DORA. Yes, Herr Doctor . . .

FREUD. Herr Professor.

DORA *nods obediently;* DORA *and* PAPA *exit,* DORA
coughing.

FREUD (*to* AUDIENCE). So. Dora. The Clinical Picture.

As you have seen . . . you are never in any danger of
corrupting an innocent girl. For where there is a genuine
ignorance of sexual matters, no hysteria can arise; and where
there are hysterical symptoms, there can no longer be any
question of 'innocence of mind'.

Of course, the question of where her knowledge came from,
continues to be a complete mystery, but not really an

important one. As the French say: 'Pour fair une omelette il faut casser des oeufs'.

FREUD. As for my use of proper terms, I again insist, 'j'appelle un chatte un chatte.' Or, in the words of the English, 'I call a pussy a pussy.'

The next part of my lecture is also a supplement to my *Interpretation of Dreams*. We will break now for ten minutes. Those among you who wish to smoke, may do so downstairs.

Bows. Goes to desk.

FREUD (*writes*). My dear Friend,

Like you, I dreamed again I was ascending a staircase, but moving rapidly and easily up the stairs, two and three at a bound. Making great progress, but I seemed to be wearing no clothes. Suddenly I noticed a woman . . . someone very young . . . but familiar . . . an acquaintance or an old family friend, perhaps . . . or perhaps a young servant . . . tripping gaily up after me . . . Seeing her, I felt suddenly paralysed, captivated, unable to move. All I could do was stand still, even though I realised she was about to overtake me. And yet, I felt not a sense of anxiety, or jealousy, or despair, as one might in waking life, but instead, I awoke in a state of almost overwhelming physical excitement.

ACT TWO

Second Dream Sequence

DORA *in night gown, locks door, checks it, sleeps.* HERR K *(played by* FREUD*) unlocks door, strolls in, stands over her, smoking. He raises covers to pull them onto* DORA, *then changes his mind, and pulls them off.*

DORA *(half-asleep).* Papa? . . . Papa, is that you? *(Sits up.)* Who's there? Hello? . . . Is somebody there? . . . Please answer if you're there . . . Hello? . . . Hello? . . . Papa!

Blackout.

FREUD'*s office – eight weeks after first session.* (*Note:* DORA *is wearing a small reticule purse attached to the clasp of her belt*).

DORA. It's always the same. There is a fire in our house. Papa is standing beside my bed and wakes me up. I get dressed quickly. Mama wants to save her jewel-case but Papa says: 'I won't let me and my two children burn to death for the sake of your jewel-case.' We hurry down stairs, and as soon as I'm outside, I wake up. But what can it mean?

FREUD. You say you dreamed it first at The Lake, several times and then again, just last night. Do you remember anything else?

DORA. No . . . I don't think so . . . But what does it mean, Herr Professor?

FREUD. What do *you* think it means?

DORA. Well, it isn't a memory, because there has never been a fire at our house. But . . . well –

FREUD. Does it make you think of anything?

DORA. Yes . . . but it can't really belong to the dream, because it just happened . . .

FREUD. No matter. Start away!

DORA. Well, Mama and Papa have been arguing again . . .

FREUD. About Frau K?

DORA. No. Mama wants to lock the dining-room door at night, so her silver is safe, and Papa wants it open, because my brother sleeps off from the dining-room, and if you lock the door, he would be locked in for the night. Mama says he's more likely to be locked out; but Papa says no: something might happen at night so that you would have to get out.

FREUD. 'Something might happen.'

DORA. Yes.

FREUD. And that made you think of fire?

DORA. Well yes, but listen! When we arrived at The Lake, there was a violent thunderstorm, and when Papa saw the little wooden house of the K's, he said he was afraid it might catch fire, because it had no lightning-rods . . . So maybe that's why I dreamed! Because each time, Papa was afraid of fire! Could that be it?

FREUD. Do you remember anything else about that first time. Anything . . . unusual . . . before or after . . .

DORA. Well, when I woke from my nap, the first day at The Lake, I saw Herr K looking at me.

FREUD. Looking at you. Perhaps you mean standing over you . . . the way your father stood over you in your dream.

DORA. No, not at all . . . and when I asked what he was doing, he said he was enjoying the view of the mountains. (A Victorian vulgar reference to 'breasts', which DORA does not understand.) So I said he could see the mountains from any window, and he said there was no need to be rude; he hoped a man could fetch things from his own bedroom.

FREUD (puzzled). His own bedroom?

DORA. Yes! And Frau K said it was true, it was his . . . So I asked for the key, just to be safe. You see, Papa and Frau K went away together every morning, leaving me all alone in the house with Herr K. But when I came back, after Herr

K's proposal, the key was gone! That's when I decided to go away with Papa! When I saw the key missing! Because I was afraid Herr K might come in and surprise me when I was dressing! So maybe the key to my dream –

FREUD. Forget the key. Your dream is simply a representation of your repressed wishes. You want to escape from Herr K. You say to yourself: 'I won't have any peace, and I won't allow myself to rest until I leave this house.' Yes?

DORA. Perhaps.

FREUD. Too simple. How do you explain this 'jewel-case' your mother wanted to save?

DORA. I don't know. Mama has quite a lot of jewels . . .

FREUD. And you?

DORA. I used to, yes, but when I found out Frau K was buying my presents instead of Papa, I gave them away.

FREUD. And what about at the time of the dream? In the dream they are arguing – do you remember your parents ever arguing about jewellery?

DORA. No . . . Yes – once! Papa and Mama fought about earrings. Mama wanted pearl drops, but Papa hates pearl drops, so he bought her a bracelet instead. And Mama was furious! She threw the bracelet at Papa and said if he was going to spend so much money on a present she didn't like, he had better just give it straight to someone who would.

FREUD. 'Someone' . . . meaning you, do you think?

DORA. Me? Oh, I don't know . . . I don't think so.

FREUD (to AUDIENCE). Note the phrase 'I don't know'. No doubt, she secretly considered herself a rival for her father's affections.

DORA (sits in FREUD's chair). I still don't see why Mama's in the dream. If it really is a dream about The Lake and Herr K and the lock, it doesn't fit at all. For one thing, Mama wasn't there, and for another – (Breaks off suddenly.) Unless maybe she thought Frau K picked the bracelet? Could that be it?

FREUD (*moves her out of the chair*). Don't try to do my job; I will explain the dream to you presently. Dora, what do you think of when I say the word 'jewel-case'.

DORA. Nothing. Oh, Herr K gave me a jewel-case for my birthday that year.

FREUD. Ahh! And what did you give him?

DORA. Nothing. It was after The Lake. I was finished with him! And besides, I had no money.

DORA *plays with reticule.*

FREUD. But perhaps Herr K also wanted a present from you? Perhaps he also wanted a little jewel-case. Do you think that is possible?

DORA. But Herr K is a man.

FREUD. Are you pretending? Dora. Do you know what it means, when we talk of a woman's jewel-case?

DORA. A case where she puts her jewels?

FREUD. Don't be coy. No one will hear you except me. You know what a woman's jewel-case could be . . . don't you. It is a favourite expression . . . like reticule . . . or purse . . . or bag . . . or box . . . it means the female genitals.

DORA (*disgusted*). I knew you would say that.

FREUD. Ah, so you knew it was so. And you know about reticules, too, don't you?

DORA. I know they're the fashion. Yes.

FREUD. The fashion, yes. And you know why, too, don't you?

DORA (*passionately*). Everything is not sex.

FREUD. Everything, no. But reticules, yes.

You've been lying on the sofa and talking, haven't you, Dora. And as you have been lying and talking, you've been playing with it – haven't you . . . You've been playing with your little reticule . . . opening it . . . shutting it . . . touching it . . . putting your finger into it . . . haven't you . . . Oh yes, Dora, I've been watching . . . I've seen what you do with your pretty little purse . . . and I know –

DORA (*fascinated*). What do you know?

FREUD (*abruptly*). The meaning of the dream is now becoming clearer. You say to yourself: 'Herr K is hunting me, he wants to force himself into my room. My jewel-case is in danger, and if anything happens, it will be Father's fault.' Lie down, please.

DORA. But Herr Professor . . . it isn't my jewel-case in my dream, it's Mama's. And Mama wasn't at the Lake. So how can you be right?

FREUD. Lie down. (DORA *obeys*.)

Precisely. Everything is opposite. You accuse your father of handing you over to Herr K; so in your dream, you dream your father is saving you from danger. Very well. Substitute 'give' for 'accept' . . . and 'withhold' for 'reject' and the dream means you are ready to give the jewel-case to Herr K because it is Herr K –

DORA (*puzzled*). But how can it be Herr K –

FREUD. Widerstand! The more you protest, the more I know it is true . . . Herr K replaces your father in the dream, just as he did in the matter of standing beside your bed, and your mother is replaced by Frau K – whom, you can't deny, was at The Lake.

This only confirms my suspicions – you've revived your old love for your father in order to protect yourself against your love for Herr K . . . because not only are you afraid of Herr K, you are afraid of yourself, and of the temptation you feel to submit.

DORA. No! . . . No! No! No! No! No!

FREUD (*takes out cigar*). Gentlemen. As I suspected, Dora resisted this part of my interpretation.

PAPA *knocks and enters*.

FREUD (*to* DORA). It's your father. Dry your eyes.

PAPA. Ah. And how is my little songbird? Have you taught her yet to perch upon your finger? Or are you still unsatisfied with her?

FREUD. No, it's been most satisfying. We're almost certain of a happy ending.

PAPA. So my treasure is opening to your little collection of picklocks, is she? Good.

FREUD. Yes, things are going quite smoothly.

PAPA. Ah. Not too smoothly, I hope. Take your time. No lady appreciates being opened with a hair pin . . . or is it a skeleton key?

FREUD. Nothing so common. But if one should have keys from elsewhere that fit . . .

PAPA (*laughs. To* DORA). Say 'Good-day'.

DORA. Yes, Papa. Good-day, Herr Professor.

FREUD (*as she turns*). Dora . . . I want you to consider what we have discussed today. Will you do that for me?

DORA *and* PAPA *exit.*

FREUD (*to* AUDIENCE). To resume.

Not surprisingly, Nora – excuse me, Dora.

(*To himself.*) Dora.

(*To* AUDIENCE.) Naturally Dora resisted my interpretation. Fortunately, even without her assistance, I made a further leap of logic, indispensable to her case, and to my own Theory of Dreams. I proposed to reveal all at the next session.

DORA *enters swinging her reticule.*

FREUD. Ah, Nora! . . . You came.

DORA. Don't I always?

FREUD. Still wearing your little reticule, I see.

DORA. Ah, Herr Professor, you see everything, don't you?

FREUD. In time, Nora, in time. Please lie down.

DORA. I think not today, Herr Professor. I have a headache.

FREUD. If you do not co-operate, I must, of course, inform your father.

DORA. Perhaps I will tell him myself . . . I think he would be very interested . . . to see what use you make of purses.

FREUD. Are you threatening me?

DORA. Not at all. I only want to show you my little birthday present from Papa . . . my little bag . . . my little reticule, as you say.

FREUD. What do you mean?

DORA. Nothing. Nothing at all. I only have brought you your fees for the month . . . The bills are very large, aren't they? . . . They fill it right to the brim . . . If we go on much longer, it will be stretched all out of shape.

FREUD. What do you mean, Dora?

DORA. What do *you* think I mean?

FREUD. Do you know what you're saying?

DORA. But look . . . Feel how soft!

FREUD (*shocked*). Dora!

(*Recovers.*) You should keep your money in your pocket.

DORA. Oh no, Herr Professor, after all, what are purses for?

FREUD. You are playing with me.

DORA. Not at all. Papa has asked me to pay you . . . and I shall . . . to please Papa . . . What, are you shy? . . . Come, come, Herr Professor . . . it won't bite, will it? . . . It's only a purse . . .

FREUD. You know very well –

DORA. Oh, I know very well you've been watching me . . . opening it . . . shutting it . . . playing with it . . . putting a finger into it . . . Oh yes, and I've been watching you watching, haven't I? And now it's time for the piper to be paid . . .

Drops reticule in FREUD'*s lap.*

(*Huskily.*) Sigi, don't bother to count . . . we both know it's all there.

Pause.

DORA (*laughs*). Herr Freud, you look so funny! Can't you take a little joke! . . .

Now what can be so important, you have to send messages to make sure I come? Don't I always? But maybe you're wrong. You see, I forgot to tell you about the smoke!

FREUD (*passes back the reticule*). Without smoke . . . there's no fire.

DORA (*together*). . . . 'there's no fire'.

FREUD. How did you know?

DORA. I'm not stupid, Herr Professor . . . You've been saying that every day for two months. You always say that. But listen; I forgot: by the Lake, Papa and Herr K smoked cigarettes, and then, after Papa left, Herr K shared one with me. And every time I woke up after the dream, I smelled smoke! (*Pause.*) Well?

FREUD. Well?

DORA. Well what do you think?

FREUD. What do *you* think, Dora?

DORA. I think Herr K had the key and was spying! What do you think?

FREUD (*takes out a cigar*). Dora. You know nothing. This – addendum – simply means you were longing for a kiss with a smoker. Herr K, perhaps.

(*To* AUDIENCE.) Gentlemen, because I am a smoker too, I came to the conclusion that she might want to have a kiss from me. Impossible to prove, of course, given the nature of Transference, but everything fits perfectly –

DORA. But why *can't* it be real smoke? Anyway, the bracelet Papa gave Mama was real.

FREUD. No it wasn't.

DORA (*indignant*). Well, what is the use of coming here, day after day, if you can only tell me things I know to be real aren't true! Why can't you tell me why I am always so tired? And why I have these terrible headaches . . . It's because of

Papa, isn't it? You can tell me . . . I won't tell anyone.

FREUD (*to* AUDIENCE). Naturally, I didn't tell her that I, too, was of the opinion that the off-spring of luetics –

DORA. Is this happening because of my father? Is this why I have trouble with my eyes? Is that why I'm always ill?

FREUD (*to* DORA). It's true your father suffers from a specific infection – a luetic aetiology, as it is more commonly known –

DORA. It's syphilis, isn't it? . . . Don't bother to lie. I heard Auntie talking when Papa had the trouble with his eyes. Mama was crying, and Auntie said 'He was ill before he married you, didn't you know' . . . Or maybe she said 'didn't you notice' . . . and then she laughed and said something else . . .

FREUD. Dora, give up this scheme to accuse your poor father. You have only yourself to blame for your illness. Your unwillingness to face –

DORA. But how can you be certain –

DORA *toys with reticule.*

FREUD. My dear, stop it. (*Slaps her hands.*) He who has eyes to see and ears to hear . . . No mortal man can keep secret from any trained observer. If your lips are silent, you're chattering away with your fingertips. Betrayal oozes out of every pore.

You complain of vaginal discharge and you say you have trouble with your eyes.

DORA. Like my Papa.

FREUD. Not like your Papa. In my experience, leucorrhoea in young girls points almost entirely to self-abuse.

DORA. Herr Professor!

FREUD. Come, come, it all adds up . . . the loss of sight, the discharge, the bedwetting, the suck-a-thumbs . . . Oh yes. I had begun to suspect masturbation even before, as soon as you mentioned bed-wetting and having gastric pains. It is well known that gastric pains and bed-wetting occur especially often in those who masturbate. It's no use, Dora. Your own case history betrays you. Confess. Confess that the illness began, not when you began to masturbate, but when you gave it up!

DORA. Herr Professor!

FREUD. My dear, the meaning of your dream is pathetically clear. You feel you are burning with love for both Herr K and your father and you want to embrace Herr K, because you are in love with him –

DORA. Herr Freud, I tell you I am not –

FREUD. Don't interrupt. You are in love with Herr K and want to embrace him, but you feel disgust because you think all men, like your father, are infected with venereal disease. All men are infected, and the pearl drop earrings are the discharge. Do you understand?

DORA (*looks at him fixedly, and says with cold calmness*). I think I'm beginning to . . . No, *you* don't interrupt . . .

Herr Freud, I loathe you. You are like a fetid lump of cheese; you leave your trail of filth and sex and slime like a great snotty slug, across everything you touch. I hate you. And I hate Papa for leaving me here. I only agreed to come because I wished to be cured, and you only talk about things which have no foundation in fact. My father has spent 32 hundred guilden, and I have come five days a week for an hour a day for the past two months, and yet you have done nothing to relieve my symptoms.

If you were a Physician, and not just a Lecturer on Nervous Diseases at the University, you would give me laudanum to alleviate my pain; if you were a Neurologist, you would try to cure us all of this loathsome disease; if you were a Father, you would protect your child from such words as I have heard, and such . . . insinuations . . .

You disgust me, Herr Freud . . . Do you hear . . . You disgust me.

DORA *exits, like 'Nora,' with dignity; Ibsenite sound of door closing.*

FREUD (*shakes his head*). Widerstand! . . . Don't worry . . .
  She will come back. They always do.

  Blackout.

Third Dream Sequence

Crystal music. DORA *enters, in Victorian nightgown like a
bridal dress, leaning on* PAPA'*s arm. Her eyes are closed.*
FREUD *plays* HERR K.

FREUD (*chants, as if in church*). Dearly beloved, let us not in
  the marriage of true minds forget Transferences. You may
  ask: What are Transferences? They are the acting out – the
  wedding as it were – the transfer, or replacement in the
  patient's mind of an earlier person by the personality of the
  doctor. In these Transferences, new editions or reprints of
  emotions and phantasies are re-awakened, and re-enacted in
  analysis.

  PAPA *hands* DORA *over to* 'HERR K'.

PAPA (*to* FREUD). You are Herr K and Papa and Herr Freud.
  You may kiss the Bride.

  'HERR K' *kisses* DORA, *hands her back to her father.*

FREUD (*to* PAPA.) You may kiss the Bride.

  PAPA *kisses her, pushes her to her knees, and into his
  groin,* FREUD *pulls her up,* PAPA *pushes her back to*
  FREUD.

PAPA. Herr Freud and Papa and Herr K and Papa and Herr
  Freud and Herr K –

  FREUD *kneels and presses his face into the folds of her
  dress.*

FREUD. We may all kiss the Bride.

PAPA. 'If any *man* can show just cause why these three may
  not be lawfully joined together, let *him* now speak, or else
  hereafter hold *his* peace'.

DORA. Will no man speak for me? (*Opens eyes.*) Will no
one . . . Mama . . . Mama, where are you . . . Mama.

Blackout. End of dream sequence.

Twelve weeks from the first session. DORA *is paler,
obviously ill.*

FREUD. You want to get well, don't you?

DORA (*coughing*). I do . . . but –

FREUD. Then trust me. Give up this senseless widerstand, this
personal resistance. Put yourself in my hands.

Now, pay attention. You said you walked round the Lake,
and when you met a man, you asked how far it was, and
when he said 'Two and a half hours,' you gave up in
despair, and returned to the boat. Is this right?

DORA. Yes.

FREUD. Ah. But last time you told me, you said the man said
'Two hours'. How do you account for this?

DORA. I don't know.

FREUD. You 'don't know'. Not good enough. You will have
to do better if you want to get well. You do want to get well,
don't you?

DORA *coughing.*

FREUD. You must learn to confront your anxieties, Dora. Now
listen: the railway station and the cemetery in your dream
are genitalia –

DORA. I knew you'd – (*Coughing fit, starts to choke.*)

FREUD. I beg your pardon.

DORA (*recovers*). I said I knew you'd say that.

FREUD. Ah. And I knew you'd say that. Let us press on. The
wood nymphs, of course, is the 'nymphae' within the thick
forest of pubic hair. Come, come. No need to be coy. You
know perfectly well 'Nymphae' means the labia minora.

DORA. Do I?

FREUD. Yes you do. You do because you have acquired your

knowledge from books. And not up-to-date ones either: old encyclopedias, I suspect, from your choice of terms. Terms so old, even doctors have trouble remembering what they mean.

DORA. But I have never seen an encyclopedia!

FREUD. Never? . . . Think hard.

DORA. No . . . yes, once, when my uncle's little boy had appendicitis.

FREUD (*to* AUDIENCE). I then remembered that Dora had also had an attack of appendicitis.

FREUD (*to* DORA) Dora, think carefully: was your own attack before or after you imagined Herr K –

DORA. I didn't imagine!

FREUD. Just answer the question.

DORA. The Lake happened in June, and I had my attack the next spring – in March, just before Papa's birthday.

FREUD. So. June, July, August . . . Nine months, then. Ahh.

DORA. Ahh? . . . what is this 'Ahh'?

FREUD. This supposed attack of appendicitis –

DORA. What do you mean, 'supposed attack'? My attack was so bad, I could not even walk. I had to learn how to walk all over again, because my right foot is still a little paralysed.

FREUD. Petite Hysteria. If we assume that you symbolically gave birth to a child nine months after The Lake, then your subsequent paralysis simply means that you regretted your 'false step' with Herr K, and still carry it with you. This fits perfectly! I can only conclude your so-called 'attack' and paralysis are simply hysterical symptoms.

DORA. It must be the wrong conclusion, Herr Professor. My so-called right foot still doesn't have any feeling.

FREUD. Widerstand. You must learn to confront unpleasant truths, Dora, or you will never get well. Admit it. Admit your ill-health is just a trick learned from Frau K. Pretty little Frau K. Adorable little Frau K with her beautiful white skin and her delicate cough. Now, to continue . . .

MAMA *knocks timidly on door*.

DORA. Oh, it's Mama . . . I must go! Happy New Year, Herr Professor.

FREUD. Ah. Very well. Ten o'clock next Monday, then?

DORA. No.

FREUD. No?

DORA. Didn't you know? I am here for the last time today.

FREUD (*hurt*). How could I know? You said nothing.

DORA. Yes. I promised myself I'd stick it out till the New Year. And now the New Year is here.

FREUD. But when did you come to this decision, Dora?

DORA. About a fortnight ago. I said to Mama 'I will give him two weeks more, but I won't wait any longer for a cure'.

FREUD. No, impossible . . . I shall speak to your Father.

DORA. I'm sorry. Herr Doctor, but Mama says –

FREUD. Who do you think I am? Do you know who I am? Do you think I'm a servant, that you can dismiss me as you please without warning? Do I look like your governess?

DORA (*laughs*). Yes . . . Well, no, not mine, but you look like the K's.

FREUD. Their governess? . . . Their new governess? This is very significant, Dora! Sit down.

DORA. No, not their *new* governess, their old one. Their old, old one. The one who had to leave two years ago because Herr K had been making violent love to her, saying he got nothing from his wife.

FREUD. Why, those are the very words you said he used with you! This is very significant, Dora. Very significant.

DORA. Well, anyway, she wanted to give two weeks warning, but when her mother heard what was happening, she told her to go away, that very day!

FREUD. Really, tell me about it.

MAMA *knocks again on door*.

DORA. Oh, I'm sorry . . . I mustn't keep Mama waiting! Good-day, Herr Professor . . . Happy New Year.

(*Note:* DORA *must not shake* FREUD'*s hand*.)

DORA *exits*.

FREUD (*as* DORA *exits*). But Dora! . . . Dora . . . Dora?

Damn you, Dora . . .

(*Shrugs*.) Ah. Gentlemen. It was obvious – Transference. She took her revenge upon me as she wanted to take her revenge on Herr K. For what better revenge than to show the world a doctor's inability to cure? . . . It was an unmistakable act of vengeance on her part – no doubt because I had neglected to discover her deep-rooted homosexual love for Frau K.

I should have suspected when I heard her first dream, which clearly warned her to leave my treatment, just as she had fled Herr K's house. I should have realised and said . . . 'Now' . . .

Gradually forgets the audience.

'Now', I should have said, 'Is there something in my treatment that reminds you of Herr K? Can you see in me any intentions similar to his? Or have you noticed anything about me which attracts you? which strikes your fancy, perhaps . . . .'

I should have said 'Dora-' . . . 'Dora!' . . . 'Dora'. Yes. 'Dora, look at me. Do I look like I have evil intentions? Or is there something – my smoking, perhaps – you especially adore or dislike? And then we could have discussed it, and perhaps the Transference would have been cleared up, and the treatment could have continued.

Instead she acted out her memories, and had her revenge on me, as she wanted to take her revenge on Herr K, and abandoned me as heartlessly as she believed herself abandoned.

And yet, I still remember her that day, listening so quietly to me, hardly contradicting me at all. And then taking my hand

in hers, smiling and wishing me well. She smiled, and
wished me well, and came no more! I knew she wouldn't.
Her father kept telling me she would, but I knew . . .

Perhaps if I had acted a part, if I'd exaggerated the value to
me of her staying on, if I'd offered her the tenderness she
longed for, I could have kept her. I do not know.

But if only I had known . . . I could have gone to her (*Sits on
couch.*) I could have said 'Dora – ' . . . 'Dora'. (*Tenderly
strokes couch.*) 'Dora . . . '

DORA *enters, aged 20.*

DORA. Herr Freud?

FREUD (*embarrassed*). Dora!

DORA. I'm sorry, I knocked. Perhaps you did not hear. If I am
   disturbing you –

FREUD. Not at all, not at all. I have a few minutes to spare
   between patients. How long has it been? Two weeks?

DORA. Two years.

FREUD. And not a day older.

DORA. Perhaps not you, Herr Freud.

FREUD. And how is the cough?

DORA. Still there . . . Yes, and I still lose my voice, and my
   right leg still drags, and sometimes . . . during migraines, I
   feel such despair . . . So you see – nothing's changed.

FREUD. Nothing?

DORA. Oh yes . . . I don't suck my thumb any more.

FREUD. And your parents?

DORA. My father is much worse, Mama is the same.

FREUD. And the K's?

   DORA *shrugs.*

FREUD. You are not still obsessed with them?

DORA. Does it matter?

FREUD. Don't say that, Dora. You should have confronted them with your feelings.

DORA. But I did . . . didn't anyone tell you? I went to Frau K, and I told her in front of everyone that I knew she was having an affair. I told her when and where and how and how long and she broke down and confessed. And Herr K was so angry, he told Frau K that he had his conquests too . . . including the proposal to me at The Lake.

FREUD (*surprised*). The proposal? He admitted it all?

DORA. He admitted enough. At least my father knew I wasn't a liar.

FREUD. And I suppose, once you had confronted them, you never saw them again?

DORA. No . . . yes . . . once. Not together. I was walking home from a lecture on Ibsen, and I saw Herr K across the square, walking the other way. Naturally, I didn't want to catch his eye, so I pulled my cloak higher, and walked past, hoping he wouldn't notice. But he did, and he turned round on the street and started to – . . . He seemed very excited.

FREUD. How do you know?

DORA (*embarrassed*). You know.

FREUD. Ah, yes, I remember. Go on.

DORA. The next thing I knew, the poor little man had walked into a carriage, and been knocked down!

FREUD. Not killed!

DORA. Oh no, just shaken. Perhaps a bit of hot air knocked out.

FREUD (*pause*). So, Dora, you look well . . . And are you happy?

DORA. Oh yes . . . my symptoms aren't too hard to live with . . . except for this paralysis, here. (*Touches the right side of her face.*) My doctor says it's luetic, but I was hoping . . . that is to say . . . you once said symptoms were not always what they seemed, and I thought, perhaps, if I could come to see you . . . perhaps . . . it might be another case of hysteria . . . and you might be able to cure me . . .

FREUD. Luetic . . . Hmmm . . . I'm very busy these days, Dora . . . preparing articles and lectures, and of course, my book on 'Dreams' has just come out. I've been appointed the Professorship at the University of Vienna . . .

DORA. Yes, I heard . . . Congratulations, Herr Professor.

FREUD. Herr *Doctor* Professor . . . Yes, well . . . I'm sorry, it seems I really have no time for you . . . And I'm afraid there is no one else sufficiently trained in the interpretation of dreams to – . . .

DORA. I understand. (*Stands; offers her hand.*) I mustn't keep you. Of course, it was only a thought. Good-day.

FREUD. Good-day, Dora. (*Kisses her hand.*)

DORA *starts to exit; pause.*

FREUD. Dora!

DORA (*turns*). Yes, Herr Freud?

FREUD. Just for my notes – I must know . . . Our last meeting – the day you decided to leave. Was it something I said? Something about me you disliked?

DORA. Of course not!

FREUD. Was it the money, was the treatment too expensive?

DORA *shakes her head.*

FREUD. Then why? Why did you stop seeing me?

DORA. Didn't you know? My father was bringing me to you so that he could spend the hour with Frau K . . .

Exits.

Epilogue – Freud Nostalgic

FREUD (*to* AUDIENCE). Years have gone by since her visit.

As for her identity, the secret of it has been kept all these years. A short while ago, I heard she had fallen ill from

other causes – accidental poisoning, I believe, and told her
physician, in private, that she had once been analysed by me
as a child. He at once, of course, recognised her as the Dora
of 1899. Excuse me, 1900.

As he assured me, no *fair* judge of analytic treatment can
reproach me for the continuation of her symptoms: aphonia,
migraine, paralysis, taedium vitae. Even so, one must not
under-value the effects of even such a fragmentary treatment
as Dora's . . . Of course, a single case could never serve to
prove such a general theory as Hysteria in Women, but it is
especially useful to study Dora in light of my *Interpretation
of Dreams*.

DORA *enters and regards* FREUD.

FREUD (*ignoring* DORA). So, Gentlemen, Dora. To sum up:
The symptoms of Hysteria are, to be frank, the sexual
activities of the patient. I can only repeat over and over
again – for I never find it otherwise – sexuality is the key to
psycho-neuroses and neuroses in general . . . And I assure
you, no one who rejects the key will ever be able to unlock
the door.

I still await critical arguments which might discredit this
theory. So far, the only rebuttals have been scurrilous ad
hominum attacks on myself, or prudish expressions of
distaste or disbelief.

FREUD *lights his final cigar.*

Gentlemen. To these, it is enough to reply in the words of
Charcot: Just because a thing is impossible – 'Ça n'empêche
pas d'exister.' Thank you. Good-night.

Clicks heels; bows.

Blackout.